Hidden Pictures

This book belongs to

_____

Birdwatching

Help Corky find 4 🐦.
Color the picture.

Berry Picking

Help Katie find 4 🍓.
Color the picture.

Where's the Paint?

Help Birdy find 4 🎨.
Color the picture.

Ribbons and Bows

Help Maria find 4 bows. Color the picture.

Reading is Fun

Help Evan find 4 📕.
Color the picture.

Making Music

Help Squeaky find 4 ♪.
Color the picture.

Ice-cream Cones

Help Billy find 5 🍦.
Color the picture.

Nectar Collector

Help the butterfly find 5 🌼.
Color the picture.

Bath Time

Help Patrick find 5 🐤.
Color the picture.

Hunt for the Hats

Help the clown find 5 🎩.
Color the picture.

Let's Go Skating

Help Sarah find 5 🧦.
Color the picture.

Find the Fish

Help the cats find 5 🐟.
Color the picture.

Raking Leaves

Help Rufus find 5 🍃.
Color the picture.

Seashells

Help Tara find 5 🐚.
Color the picture.

Find the Birds

Help the scarecrow find 5 🐦.
Color the picture.

Turnips Tonight!

Help Piggy find 5 🥕.
Color the picture.

Bedtime

Help Mr. Mouse find 6 🛏. Color the picture.

Lost Mittens

Help Peg find 6 🧤.
Color the picture.

Beans Tonight!

Help the cowboys find 6 🫘.
Color the picture.

Paper Airplanes

Help Sachi find 6 ✈.
Color the picture.

Planting Flowers

Help Fuzzy Bear find 6 🌷.
Color the picture.

Gingerbread

Help Mrs. Green find 6 🍪.
Color the picture.

Don't Forget the Cups!

Help Jake find 7 cups.
Color the picture.

Find the Bones

Help the pups find 7 bones.
Color the picture.

Playing Golf

Help Thumper find 7 ◯.
Color the picture.

Remove the bookmark and sign pages from the book. Make the bookmark and the sign or help your child make them.

Pull-Out Bonus Activities
Owl Bookmark and Sign

Oliver Owl Bookmark

Directions

- Color and cut out the bookmark.
- Cut along the dotted line on Oliver Owl's beak. (It's easier to do this if you fold Oliver.) Hook Oliver's beak over the page to mark your place.

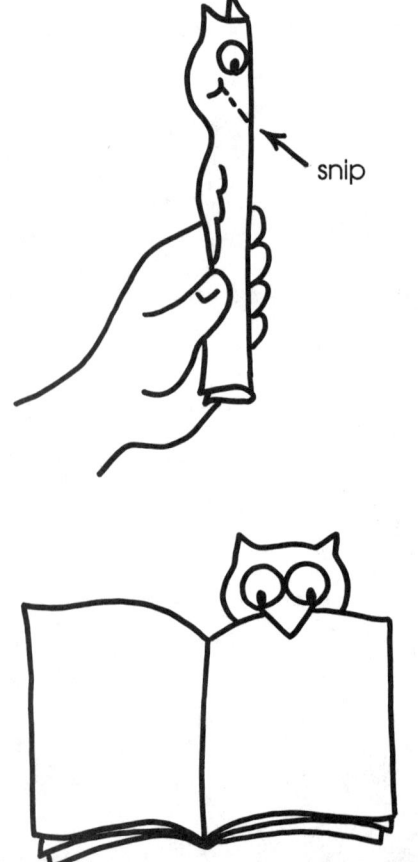

snip

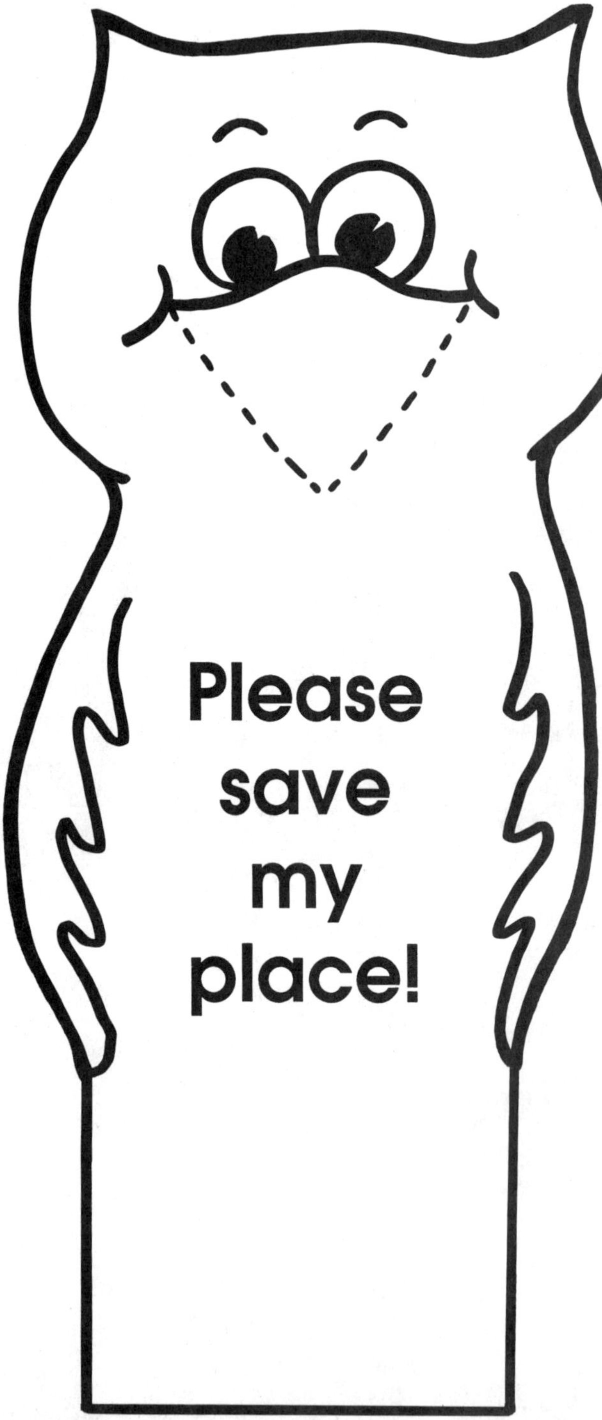

Please save my place!

Doorknob Sign

Color and cut out this handy sign. Hang it on your doorknob when you are working.

Shhh. I'm working.

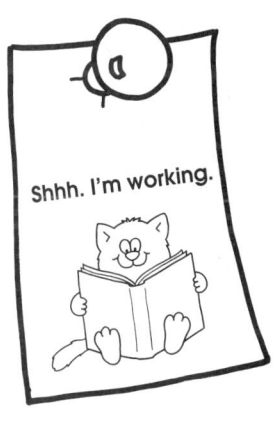

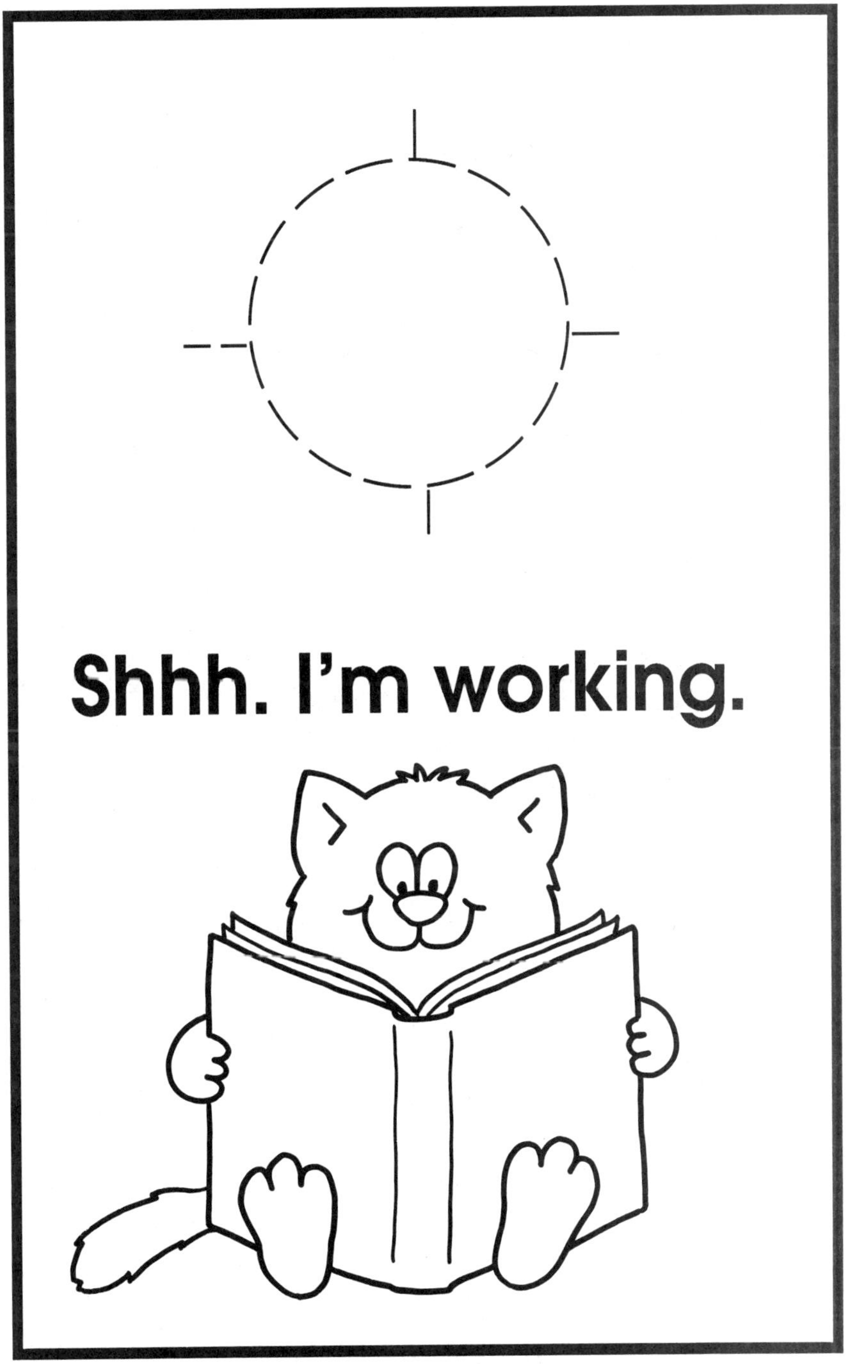
Shhh. I'm working.

© Frank Schaffer Publications, Inc.

Summer Fun

Help Sunny find 7 🪣.
Color the picture.

Looking for Ladybugs

Help Tony find 7 🐞.
Color the picture.

Nuts!

Help Bushy Squirrel find 7 🥜.
Color the picture.

Who's Eating the Leaves?

Help Pam find 7 🐌.
Color the picture.

Brush Your Teeth

Help Smiley find 7 🖌.
Color the picture.

Rattles!

Help the baby find 8 🪇.
Color the picture.

Rabbits

Help the magician find 8 🐇.
Color the picture.

Swiss Cheese

Help Merry Mouse find 8 🧀.
Color the picture.

Blowing Bubbles

Help Kim find 8 ◯.
Color the picture.

Letters

Help the mailman find 8 ✉. Color the picture.

Apples

Help the hungry horse find 8 🍎.
Color the picture.

Coloring Time

Help Keith find 9 ✏️.
Color the picture.

Bake a Cake

Help the chef find 9 ◯.
Color the picture.

Hunt and Peck

Help Rusty Rooster find 9 🌽.
Color the picture.

Bugs in the Bog

Help Leaping Lizzie find 9 🐝.
Color the picture.

Honeybees

Help Baby Bear find 9 🐝.
Color the picture.

Where's My Popcorn?

Help Lee find 9 🍿.
Color the picture.

Tea Time

Help the teapot find 9 🍵.
Color the picture.

Yummy Worms

Help Chirpy find 10 🪱.
Color the picture.

Carrot Surprise

Help the bunny find 10 🥕.
Color the picture.

Baseball

Help Slugger find 10 ⚾.
Color the picture.

Go Bananas

Help the gorilla find 10 🍌.
Color the picture.

Birthday Cake

Help Brett find 10 🕯.
Color the picture.

The Piggy Bank

Help Rosa find 10 coins.
Color the picture.

Put a Cherry on Top

Help Cory find 10 🍒.
Color the picture.

Look for These Pictures!

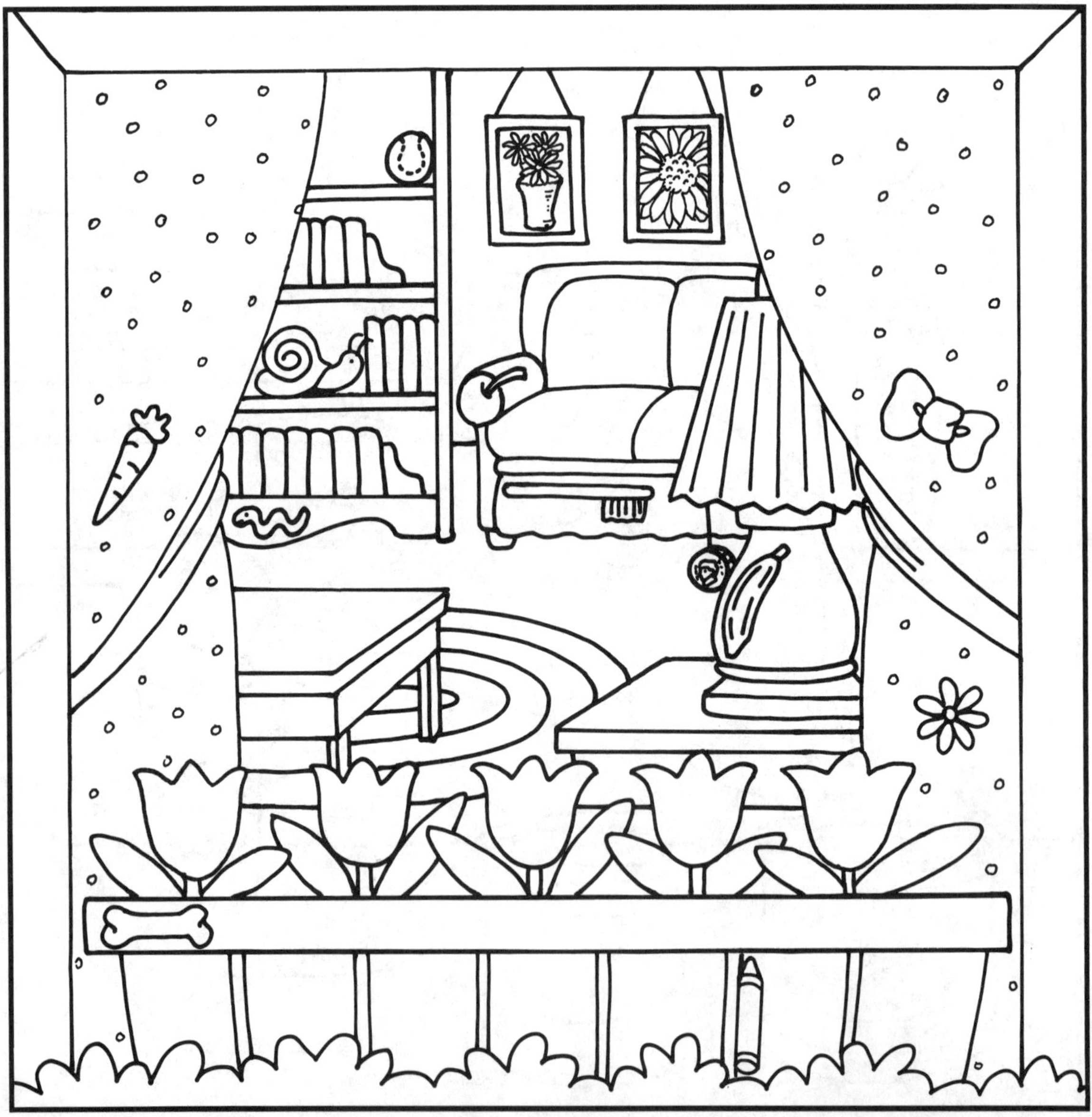